THE SMART WORDS AND WICKED WIT OF WINSTON CHURCHILL

Max Morris

THE SMART WORDS AND WICKED WIT OF WINSTON CHURCHILL

Max Morris

Skyhorse Publishing
A Herman Graf Book

Copyright © Summersdale Publishers Ltd, 2016
Published by arrangement with Summersdale Publishers Ltd.
First Skyhorse Publishing edition 2017

Skyhorse Publishing books may be purchased in bulk at special discounts
for sales promotion, corporate gifts, fund-raising, or educational purposes.
Special editions can also be created to specifications. For details, contact the
Special Sales Department, Skyhorse Publishing, 307 West 36th Street, 11th
Floor, New York, NY 10018 or info@skyhorsepublishing.com.

Skyhorse® and Skyhorse Publishing® are registered trademarks of Skyhorse
Publishing, Inc.®, a Delaware corporation.

Visit our website at www.skyhorsepublishing.com.

10 9 8 7 6

Library of Congress Cataloging-in-Publication Data is available on file.

Image credit: iStock

Print ISBN: 978-1-5107-1582-0
Ebook ISBN: 978-1-5107-1585-1

Printed in China

CONTENTS

DOMESTIC POLITICS

The Admiralty has demanded six, The Treasury said we could only have four so we compromised on eight.

ON THE FINER POINTS OF
DEFENCE PROCUREMENT

—◆—

A love of tradition has never weakened a nation, indeed it has strengthened nations in their hour of peril; but the new view must come, the world must roll forward... Let us have no fear of the future.

1944

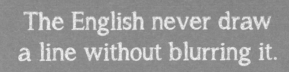

The English never draw
a line without blurring it.

I see it is said that leaders should keep their ears to the ground. All I can say is that the British nation will find it very hard to look up to the leaders who are detected in that somewhat ungainly posture.

———◆———

Don't get torpedoed; for if I am left alone your colleagues will eat me.

LETTER TO THEN PM DAVID LLOYD GEORGE WHO WAS VISITING RUSSIA, 1916

Reconstructing a
Cabinet is like solving
a kaleidoscopic
jigsaw puzzle.

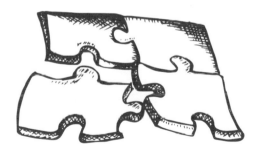

An announcement of a prospective
surplus is always a milestone in a budget.

———◆———

Everyone threw blame on me. I have
noticed that they nearly always do.
I suppose it is because they think
I shall be able to bear it best.

ON STANDING AS A CANDIDATE FOR
ELECTION TO THE HOUSE OF COMMONS
FOR THE FIRST TIME AND LOSING

———◆———

If this is a blessing,
it is certainly very
well disguised.

AFTER HIS ELECTION DEFEAT, 1945

Their will was resolute and remorseless,
and as it proved, unconquerable.
It fell to me to express it.

ON THE BRITISH PEOPLE

———◆———

The British nation is unique in this
respect: they are the only people
who like to be told how bad things
are, who like to be told the worst.

1941

———◆———

We shall not be judged by the
criticisms of our opponents but by
the consequences of our acts.

PONDERING POLITICS

Politics is the ability to foretell what is going to happen tomorrow, next week, next month and next year. And to have the ability afterwards to explain why it didn't happen.

———◆———

For my own part I have always felt that a politician is to be judged by the animosities which he excites among his opponents. I have always set myself not merely to relish but to deserve thoroughly their censure.

It would be a great reform in politics if wisdom could be made to spread as easily and as rapidly as folly.

The inherent vice of capitalism is the unequal sharing of blessings. The inherent virtue of socialism is the equal sharing of miseries.

———◆———

Courage is what it takes to stand up and speak; courage is also what it takes to sit down and listen.

———◆———

The whole history of the world is summed up in the fact that when nations are strong they are not always just, and when they wish to be just they are often no longer strong.

HOUSE OF COMMONS MARCH 26, 1936

An appeaser is
one who feeds a
crocodile – hoping it
will eat him last.

To think you can make a man richer by putting on a tax is like a man standing in a bucket and trying to pull himself up by the handles.

———◆———

All the greatest things are simple, and many can be expressed in a single word: freedom; justice; honour; duty; mercy; hope.

Change is agreeable to the human
mind, and gives satisfaction,
sometimes short-lived, to ardent
and anxious public opinion.

—◆—

The best argument against democracy
is a five-minute conversation
with the average voter.

—◆—

I don't see any way of realising our
hopes for a world organisation in six
days. Even the Almighty took seven.

TO ROOSEVELT ON THE LIKELY DURATION OF THE
YALTA CONFERENCE WITH STALIN, 1945

He is asked to stand, he wants to sit, he is expected to lie.

THE DEFINITION OF A PARLIAMENTARY CANDIDATE

Things do not get better by being let
alone. Unless they are adjusted, they
explode with a shattering detonation.

———◆———

Democracy is more vindictive
than Cabinets.

———◆———

Never hold discussions with the monkey
when the organ grinder is in the room.

ON DISCUSSIONS WITH MUSSOLINI AND HIS
FOREIGN MINISTER

WAR AND PEACE

The problems of victory are more
agreeable than those of defeat,
but they are no less difficult.

1942

———◆———

We must always be ready to make
sacrifices for the great causes; only in that
way shall we live to keep our souls alive.

———◆———

The best evidence of the fairness
of any settlement is the fact that
it fully satisfies neither party.

In wartime, truth is so
precious that she should
always be attended by
a bodyguard of lies.

1943

We have not journeyed all this way across the centuries, across the oceans, across the mountains, across the prairies, because we are made of sugar candy.

———◆———

Now this is not the end. It is not even the beginning of the end. But it is, perhaps, the end of the beginning.

Nothing is more costly,
nothing is more sterile, than vengeance.

———◆———

If Hitler invaded Hell, I would make
at least a favourable reference to the
Devil in the House of Commons.

———◆———

When you have to
kill a man it costs nothing
to be polite.

ON THE PUBLIC'S RESPONSE TO HIS
FORMAL AND COURTEOUS LETTER
DECLARING WAR WITH JAPAN, 1941

Any clever person
can make plans for
winning a war if he
has no responsibility
for carrying them out.

1946

How many wars have been precipitated by firebrands! How many misunderstandings which led to wars could have been removed by temporising! How often have countries fought cruel wars and then after a few years found themselves not only friends but allies!

———◆———

If you go on with this nuclear arms race, all you are going to do is make the rubble bounce.

It is dangerous to meddle with Admirals
when they say they can't do things.
They have always got the weather or
fuel or something to argue about.

———◆———

It is better to perish
than to live as slaves.

———◆———

To build may have to be the
slow and laborious task of
years. To destroy can be the
thoughtless act of a single day.

One day President Roosevelt
told me that he was asking
publicly for suggestions
about what the war should
be called. I said at once
'The Unnecessary War'.

The statesman who yields to war fever must realise that once the signal is given, he is no longer the master of policy but the slave of unforeseeable and uncontrollable events.

———◆———

Never give in. Never give in. Never, never, never, never – in nothing, great or small, large or petty – never give in, except to convictions of honour and good sense. Never yield to force. Never yield to the apparently overwhelming might of the enemy.

SAGE ADVICE

Stilton and port are like man and wife. They should never be separated. 'Whom God has joined together, let no man put asunder.'

———◆———

The greatest lesson in life is to know that even fools are right sometimes.

———◆———

Never stand so high upon a principle that you cannot lower it to suit the circumstances.

Courage is rightly esteemed the first of human qualities because it has been said; it is the quality which guarantees all others.

———◆———

Every day you make progress. Every step may be fruitful. Yet there will stretch out before you an ever-lengthening, ever-ascending, ever-improving path. You know you will never get to the end of the journey. But this, so far from discouraging, only adds to the joy and the glory of the climb.

It is better to be making
the news than taking
it, to be an actor
rather than a critic.

There is always much to be said for not attempting more than you can do and for making a certainty of what you try. But this principle, like others in life and war, has its exceptions.

———◆———

Every man should ask himself each day whether he is not too readily accepting negative solutions.

What you say is very grandfatherly. You're always giving me grandfatherly advice. You're not my grandfather, you know.

TO HIS SON RANDOLF

——◆——

In finance, everything that is agreeable is unsound and everything that is sound is disagreeable.

——◆——

Dogs look up to you, cats look down on you. Give me a pig – he just looks you in the eye and treats you as an equal.

It is not enough that
we do our best;
sometimes we have to
do what is required.

Nourish your hopes, but do
not overlook realities.

———◆———

It is a fine thing to be honest, but it
is also very important to be right.

———◆———

How little we should worry
about anything except doing our best.

CHURCHILL
ON
CHURCHILL

All I can say is I have taken more out of
alcohol than alcohol has taken out of me.

I realised that I must be on my best
behaviour: punctual, subdued, reserved,
in short display all the qualities
with which I am least endowed.

ON DINING WITH THE
PRINCE OF WALES IN 1896

We are all worms. But I do
believe I am a glow-worm.

Dead birds don't fall out of their nest.

**ON BEING INFORMED THAT
HIS FLY WAS UNDONE**

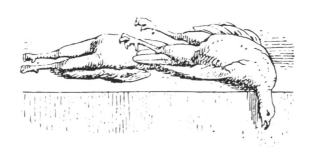

I earned my livelihood by dictating
articles which had a wide circulation…
I lived in fact from mouth to hand.

———◆———

I am ready to meet my Maker.
Whether my Maker is prepared
for the great ordeal of meeting
me is another matter.

———◆———

For myself I am an optimist –
It does not seem to be much
use being anything else.

I am a sporting man.
I always give them a fair
chance to get away.

ON WHY HE OFTEN MISSED
TRAINS AND AEROPLANES

———◆———

When I look back on all these
worries I remember the story
of the old man who said on his
deathbed that he had had a
lot of trouble in his life, most of
which had never happened.

I pass with relief
from the tossing sea
of Cause and Theory
to the firm ground
of Result and Fact.

I decline utterly to be impartial as between the fire brigade and the fire.

RESPONDING TO CLAIMS THAT HIS EDITING OF *THE BRITISH GAZETTE* DURING THE GENERAL STRIKE WAS BIASED

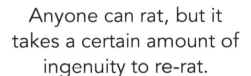

Anyone can rat, but it takes a certain amount of ingenuity to re-rat.

ON RE-JOINING THE CONSERVATIVES 20 YEARS AFTER LEAVING THEM FOR THE LIBERALS

Asking me not to make a
speech is like asking a centipede to get
along and not put a foot on the ground.

———◆———

I could not live without
champagne. In victory I deserve
it. In defeat I need it.

———◆———

No, I didn't say it; but I'm sorry I didn't,
because it was quite witty… and so true.

CHURCHILL ON ONE OF HIS MANY MISATTRIBUTED
QUOTES

PEOPLE

Often in the casual remarks of great men one learns their true mind in an intimate way.

———◆———

It is hard, if not impossible, to snub a beautiful woman – they remain beautiful and the rebuke recoils.

———◆———

One always measures friendships by how they show up in bad weather.

Now Clemmie will have
to be a lady at last.

— ◆ —

When the eagles are silent, the
parrots begin to jabber.

— ◆ —

This is one of those cases in which the
imagination is baffled by the facts.

Lovely, inspiring. All the
film people in the world if
they had scoured the globe
could not have found anyone
so suited to the part.

ON QUEEN ELIZABETH II

I understood definitely that he had blown up all sorts of things and was therefore a very great man.

ON OLIVER CROMWELL

———◆———

Rare and precious is the truly disinterested man.

———◆———

Who was Socrates, anyhow? A very argumentative Greek who had a nagging wife and was finally compelled to commit suicide because he was a nuisance! Still, he was beyond doubt a considerable person.

I then had one of the three or four long intimate conversations with him which are all I can boast.

ON HIS FATHER

At his best he could almost
talk a bird out of a tree.

ON DAVID LLOYD GEORGE

———◆———

Meeting Roosevelt was like uncorking
your first bottle of champagne.

———◆———

I hate nobody except Hitler –
and that is professional.

It is the habit of the boa constrictor to besmear the body of his victim with a foul slime before he devours it; and there are many people in England, and perhaps elsewhere, who seem to be unable to contemplate military operations for clear political objects, unless they can cajole themselves into the belief that their enemy are utterly and hopelessly vile.

We have always found the Irish a bit odd. They refuse to be English.

———◆———

I want no criticism of America at my table. The Americans criticise themselves more than enough.

POWER

One mark of a great man is the
power of making lasting impressions
upon people he meets.

The empires of the future are
the empires of the mind.

Dictators ride to and fro on tigers
from which they dare not dismount.
And the tigers are getting hungry.

1938

Money is like manure;
it's only good if you
spread it around.

You don't make the poor richer
by making the rich poorer.

—◆—

The finest combination in the world is
power and mercy. The worst combination
in the world is weakness and strife.

—◆—

A fanatic is one who can't change his
mind and won't change the subject.

Si vous m'obstaclerez, je vous liquiderai.
(If you obstacle me, I will liquidate you.)

TO CHARLES DE GAULLE, 1943

———◆———

Perhaps it is better to be
irresponsible and right than to
be responsible and wrong.

———◆———

But on the whole it is wise
in human affairs, and in the
government of men, to separate
pomp from power.

As long as the job
is done, it does not
matter much who
gets the credit.

No one pretends that democracy is perfect or all-wise. Indeed, it has been said that democracy is the worst form of government except all those other forms that have been tried from time to time.

———◆———

It is wonderful how well men can keep secrets they have not been told.

Always be on guard
against tyranny, whatever
shape it may assume.

———◆———

Strength is granted to
us all when we are needed
to serve great causes.

———◆———

Healthy citizens are the
greatest asset any
country can have.

Everyone is in favour of free speech... but some people's idea of it is that they are free to say what they like, but if anyone else says anything back, that is an outrage.

THE
FRONT
LINE

We are waiting for the
long-promised invasion. So are the fishes.

1940

When danger is far off we
may think of our weakness;
when it is near we must not
forget our strength.

1939

Learn to get used to it.
Eels get used to skinning.

ON BOMBING, 1940

It was the nation and the race dwelling all round the globe that had the lion's heart: I had the luck to be called upon to give the roar.

There is only one thing worse
than fighting with allies, and that
is fighting without them.

1945

—◆—

The flying peril is not a peril
from which one can fly. It is
necessary to face it where we
stand. We cannot possibly retreat.
We cannot move London.

—◆—

You must put your head in the
lion's mouth if the performance
is to be a success.

ON HIS EXPERIENCES IN THE SECOND BOER WAR,
19 FEBRUARY 1900

If one has to submit it is
wasteful not to do so with
the best grace possible.

——◆——

We shall go on to the end, we shall
fight in France, we shall fight on the
seas and oceans, we shall fight with
growing confidence and growing
strength in the air, we shall defend
our Island, whatever the cost may
be. We shall fight on the beaches,
we shall fight on the landing
grounds, we shall fight in the fields
and in the streets, we shall fight in
the hills; we shall never surrender.

AFTER THE EVACUATION FROM DUNKIRK, 1940

A remarkable and definite
victory. The bright gleam
has caught the helmets of
our soldiers and warmed
and cheered all our hearts.

1942

You ask, what is our aim? I can answer in one word. It is victory, victory at all costs, victory in spite of all terror, victory, however long and hard the road may be; for without victory, there is no survival.

FIRST SPEECH AS PRIME MINISTER IN THE HOUSE OF COMMONS, 1940

———◆———

Let us therefore brace ourselves to our duties, and so bear ourselves that if the British Empire and its Commonwealth last for a thousand years, men will still say, 'This was their finest hour.'

1940

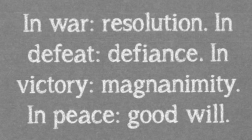

These are not dark days: these are great days – the greatest days our country has ever lived.

———◆———

We must all turn our backs upon the horrors of the past. We must look to the future. We cannot afford to drag forward across the years that are to come the hatreds and revenges which have sprung from the injuries of the past.

He hopes, by killing large numbers of civilians, and women and children, that he will terrorise and cow the people of this mighty imperial city... Little does he know the spirit of the British nation, or the tough fibre of the Londoners.

DURING THE BLITZ, 1940

STRUGGLES AND STRIFE

Success consists of going
from failure to failure without
loss of enthusiasm.

———◆———

There are a terrible lot of lies
going about the world, and the
worst is that half of them are true.

———◆———

We have a lot of anxieties,
and one cancels out
another very often.

1943

In Russia a man is called reactionary if he objects to having his property stolen and his wife and children murdered.

—◆—

It is much better to set up an objective, even if it be beyond your reach, than it is to give up the struggle at the outset.

One ought never to turn
one's back on threatened
danger and try to run away
from it. If you do that you
will double the danger. But
if you meet it promptly and
without flinching, you will
reduce the danger by half.

Out of intense
complexities, intense simplicities emerge.

———◆———

Dangers which are warded off and
difficulties which are overcome
before they reach a crisis are
utterly unrecognised. Eaten
bread is soon forgotten.

1919

———◆———

Nothing in life is so
exhilarating as to be shot
at without result.

It is never necessary to commit suicide,
especially when you may live to regret it.

ON MAKING CONCESSIONS IN
PARLIAMENT TO AVERT DEFEAT

———◆———

Woe betide the leaders now perched
on their dizzy pinnacles of triumph
if they cast away at the conference
table what the soldiers had won on a
hundred blood-soaked battlefields.

———◆———

We are still masters of our fate.
We are still captains of our souls.

Kites rise highest
against the wind
– not with it.

It is easier to break crockery
than to mend it.

———◆———

The power of the Executive to
cast a man into prison without
formulating any charge known
to the law and particularly to
deny him the judgement of his
peers is in the highest degree
odious and is the foundation
of all totalitarian government
whether Nazi or Communist.

EDUCATION

Young man on seeing Churchill leaving the bathroom without washing his hands: At Eton they taught us to wash our hands after using the toilet. **Churchill:** At Harrow they taught us not to piss on our hands.

—◆—

The first duty of the university is to teach wisdom, not a trade; character not technicalities. We want a lot of engineers in the modern world, but we do not want a world of engineers.

Perhaps no one has ever passed
so few examinations and
received so many degrees.

ON RECEIVING ONE OF HIS MANY
HONORARY DEGREES

———◆———

For years I thought my father,
with his experience and flair, had
discerned in me the qualities of
military genius. But I was told
later that he had only come to
the conclusion that I was not
clever enough to go to the bar.

It is a good thing for an
uneducated man to read
books of quotations.

But now I pity undergraduates, when I see what frivolous lives many of them lead in the midst of precious fleeting opportunity. After all, a man's life must be nailed to a cross either of Thought or Action.

———◆——

Criticism may not be agreeable, but it is necessary. It fulfils the same function as pain in the human body. It calls attention to an unhealthy state of things.

It is not pleasant to feel oneself so completely outclassed and left behind at the very beginning of the race.

ON STARTING SCHOOL

I had a feeling once about Mathematics, that I saw it all – Depth beyond Depth was revealed to me… It was like politics. But it was after dinner, and I let it go!

———◆———

Where my reason, imagination or interest were not engaged, I would not or I could not learn.

———◆———

These examinations were a great trial to me… I should have liked to be asked to say what I knew. They always tried to ask what I did not know.

INTERESTS,
DISINTERESTS
AND LOVES

A day away from Chartwell
is a day wasted.

———◆———

No hour of life is lost that is
spent in the saddle.

———◆———

Like chasing a quinine pill
around a cow pasture.

ON GOLF

When I get to heaven I mean to
spend a considerable portion of my
first million years painting, and so
get to the bottom of the subject.

———◆———

I prefer landscapes.
A tree doesn't complain that
I haven't done it justice.

ON PAINTING

———◆———

I cannot pretend to feel impartial
about the colours. I rejoice with the
brilliant ones, and I am genuinely
sorry for the poor browns.

Writing a book is an adventure. To begin with, it is a toy and an amusement; then it becomes a mistress, and then it becomes a master, and then a tyrant. The last phase is that... you kill the monster, and fling him out to the public.

Study history, study history.
In history lies all the secrets of statecraft.

———◆———

When I was younger I made it a
rule never to take strong drink
before lunch. It is now my rule
never to do so before breakfast.

———◆———

I get my exercise serving as pall-
bearer to my many friends who
exercised all their lives.

If I could not be who I am,
I would most like to be Mrs
Churchill's second husband.

———◆———

She shone for me like the
evening star. I loved her dearly
– but at a distance.

ON HIS MOTHER

———◆———

How can I tell that my temper would have
been as sweet or my companionship
as agreeable if I had abjured from
my youth the goddess Nicotine?

Where does the family start? It starts with a young man falling in love with a girl – no superior alternative has yet been found.

My most brilliant achievement
was my ability to be able to
persuade my wife to marry me.

———◆———

My rule of life prescribed as an
absolutely sacred rite the smoking
of cigars and also the drinking
of alcohol before, after, and if
need be during all meals and in
the intervals between them.

PHILOSOPHY

A hopeful disposition is not the sole
qualification to be a prophet.

—◆—

We are happier in many ways when we
are old than when we are young. The
young sow wild oats, the old grow sage.

—◆—

There is nothing wrong in change,
if it is in the right direction.
To improve is to change.

We shape our buildings,
and afterwards our
buildings shape us.

Everyone has his day,
and some days last
longer than others.

What is the use of living, if it
be not to strive for noble causes
and to make this muddled world a better
place to live in after we are gone?

Death is the greatest gift that
God has made to us.

1943

You will make all kinds of
mistakes; but as long as you
are generous and true, and also
fierce, you cannot hurt the world
or even seriously distress her.

———◆———

It is a mistake to look too far
ahead. Only one link in the chain of
destiny can be handled at a time.

One ought to be just
before one is generous.

Some people will deny anything.
But there are some denials
that do not alter the facts.

Nothing should be done for spite's sake.

Sometimes when [Fortune] scowls
most spitefully, she is preparing
her most dazzling gifts.

Without work
there is no play.

Too often the strong, silent
man is silent only because he
does not know what to say, and
is reputed strong only because
he has remained silent.

When you have to hold a hot coffee pot,
it is better not to break the handle off.

1944

Usually youth is for freedom
and reform, maturity for
judicious compromise, and old
age for stability and repose.

No folly is more costly than the
folly of intolerant idealism.

A woman is as old as she looks;
a man is as old as he feels; and a
boy is as old as he is treated.

When you get a thing the way
you want it, leave it alone.

… live dangerously;
take things as they come;
dread naught, all will be well.

———◆———

The glory of light cannot exist
without its shadows.

———◆———

Difficulties mastered are
opportunities won.

WORDS SAID AND UNSAID

Men will forgive a man
anything except bad prose.

———◆———

What if, instead of 'We shall fight on
the beaches', I had said, 'Hostilities
will be engaged with our adversary
on the coastal perimeter'?

ON THE IMPORTANCE OF
WELL-WRITTEN SPEECHES

You are very free with your commas.
I always reduce them to a minimum:
and use 'and' or an 'or' as a
substitute not as an addition.

———◆———

Don't argue the matter.
The difficulties will argue for themselves.

———◆———

Men occasionally stumble over the truth,
but most of them pick themselves up and
hurry off as if nothing had happened.

The Times is speechless,
and takes three
columns to express
its speechlessness.

This is the sort of English up
with which I will not put.

ON BEING CORRECTED ON HIS USE
OF PREPOSITIONS

Broadly speaking, the short words
are the best, and the old words,
when short, are best of all.

I got into my bones the essential structure of the ordinary British sentence, which is a noble thing.

———◆———

We are masters of the unsaid words, but slaves of those we let slip out.

———◆———

In the art of drafting [income tax law] there seems to be a complete disdain of the full stop, and even the humble colon is an object to be avoided.

In a sensible language like English important words are connected and related to another by other little words. The Romans in that stern antiquity considered such a method weak and unworthy.

If you have an important point to make, don't try to be subtle or clever. Use the pile driver. Hit the point once. Then come back and hit it again. Then hit it a third time; a tremendous whack.

———◆———

Perhaps we have been guilty of some terminological inexactitudes.

In the course of my life I have often had to eat my words, and I must confess that I have always found it a wholesome diet.

A CUTTING TONGUE

He has… the gift of compressing the largest amount of words into the smallest amount of thought.

ON RAMSAY MACDONALD

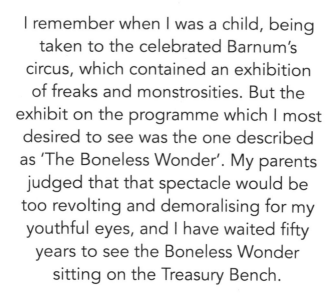

I remember when I was a child, being taken to the celebrated Barnum's circus, which contained an exhibition of freaks and monstrosities. But the exhibit on the programme which I most desired to see was the one described as 'The Boneless Wonder'. My parents judged that that spectacle would be too revolting and demoralising for my youthful eyes, and I have waited fifty years to see the Boneless Wonder sitting on the Treasury Bench.

ON RAMSAY MACDONALD

A modest man who has much to be modest about.

ON CLEMENT ATTLEE

He looks like a female
llama who has just been
surprised in her bath.

ON CHARLES DE GAULLE

———◆———

Baldwin was a remarkable
man. I like to make people
do what I wish. Baldwin liked
to do what they wanted.

———◆———

Like the grub that feeds
on the Royal Jelly and
thinks it's a Queen Bee.

ON CLEMENT ATTLEE

He is the only case I know of a bull who carries around his own china shop with him.

ON JOHN FOSTER DULLES, US SECRETARY OF STATE

I always hate to compare Napoleon
with Hitler, as it seems an insult
to the great Emperor and warrior
to connect him in any way with a
squalid caucus boss and butcher.

———◆———

He had all the virtues I dislike and
none of the vices I admire.

ON STAFFORD CRIPPS

———◆———

His chest is a cage in which two squirrels
are at war – his conscience and his career.

ON STAFFORD CRIPPS

I have never seen a human being who more perfectly represented the modern concept of a robot.

ON RUSSIAN POLITICIAN
VYACHESLAV MOLOTOV

———◆———

A prisoner of war is a man who tries to kill you and fails, and then asks you not to kill him.

He is a foul-weather friend.

ON LORD BEAVERBROOK

This cat does more for the war effort than you do. He acts as a hot-water bottle and saves fuel and power.

TO RAB BUTLER

———◆———

I do not challenge the honourable gentlemen when the truth leaks out of him from time to time.

ON BEING INTERRUPTED BY
EMANUEL SHINWELL,
A LABOUR POLITICIAN